Taking The Bull By The Horns

By J P Miller

Copyright

Your Gift

'As a special 'Thank you' for purchasing my book and to help you further with your Money Personality education, here's a gift for you – with my compliments!

It's free video training called 'Master Your Money' where you will get further insights into Your Money Personality plus learn how to build your financial foundations – the key to a secure financial future.

It's valued at $97 but it's yours – as my gift.'

You can access it here:

http://yourlifeyourmoney.com.au

Contents

Foreword

Before we start looking at Your Money Personality and why knowing Your Money Personality will change your life, I just want to introduce myself and answer that age old question you're probably asking - "Why on earth should I read this Book?"

I've lived this stuff! Maybe that's why I'm so passionate about researching and developing this profiling process. After graduating with a Bachelor of Business (Accounting) degree, I started my professional life as an accountant with a multi-national accounting firm – Delloites. I learned heaps on the job, some of it not really anything to do with accounting! The most valuable thing I learned during this time was that sitting in an office, checking up on other people's work was definitely not for me! Even then, it took me quite a few more years to get to a point where I just had to leave – or die. I know that's pretty strong stuff, but with this research I'm doing, it's just so clear that if you're not in the right job earning in the way that's right for you – for your money personality type – then that's exactly how it feels.

Have you found that? Have you felt that you just had to get out of your job – and that if you didn't, you would either explode, or pass out?

Do you wonder how you're going to get out of that "Rat Race" and move into something that makes your heart sing?

Well, wonder no more! In this book, I will introduce you to Your Money Personality. You'll get a feel for the best ways you can move forward in the areas of:

1. Earning,
2. Spending,
3. Saving,
4. Investing, and
5. Giving.

You'll find out what Money Personality Animal Archetype you are – a Bull, a Bear, an Owl or a Dolphin!

Each one of these "personalities" looks at, and thinks about, money and investing in very different ways. Even their money management is different.

Just imagine how good you will feel when you know what your financial strengths are – and you know how to utilize them to your best advantage. Think how empowering it will be to understand your money challenges and then learn how to manage them!

Disclaimers

Exclusion of liability

All Money Matters Pty Ltd (AMM) and its officers are independent of any vested interest. It/they is not affiliated with any stockbroker, unit or investment trust, insurance agency or other financial organisation of any type. It makes no financial offerings of any kind and has no salespersons or agents.

This eBook is designed to provide information only and is not providing any recommendation to purchase any investment that may be described. While the author and All Money Matters Pty Ltd have taken all reasonable care in the preparation of this eBook, its accuracy cannot be warranted. Materials and examples given do not constitute advice on the making or changing of any particular investment.

If financial advice or other expert investing assistance is required, the services of a licensed professional advisor should be sought. For these reasons the author and All Money Matters will not be liable for any loss arising from investments made or changed in reliance on statements contained in this eBook.

AMM, and its officers, are not recommending any investment which may be described in this eBook nor do they have any financial interest or receive any financial benefit, unless specifically declared.

Intellectual Property

Copyright

All Money Matters Pty Ltd (AMM) is the copyright owner of all text, graphics and activities contained in this eBook, except as otherwise indicated. Other parties' graphics and/ or trademarks and service marks that may be referred to herein are the property of their respective owners.

You may print a copy of the information contained in this eBook for your personal use only, but you must not reproduce or distribute the text, graphics or activities to others or substantially copy the information on your own server without prior written permission of AMM.

You may use text, provided that:
The copyright notice appears in all copies and that both the copyright and this permission notice appear;

Use and reproduction of documents, information and related graphics available from the eBook is limited to personal, non-commercial use;

No documents or related graphics, including logos, available from the eBook or website are modified in any way; and

No graphics, including logos, available from the eBook or website are used separate from accompanying text.

Subject to the provisions of the Copyright Act 1968 (Cth), use or reproduction for any other purpose than as authorised by these terms and conditions is expressly prohibited.

Trademarks
Except where otherwise specified, any word or device to which is attached the ™ or ® symbol is a registered trademark.

If you use any of our trade marks in reference to AMM's activities, products or services, you must include a statement attributing that trade mark to AMM. You must not use any of AMM's trademarks:

In or as the whole or part of your own trademarks;

In connection with activities, products or services which are not ours;

In a manner which may be confusing, misleading or deceptive;

In a manner that disparages us or our information, products or services (including this eBook and all AMM's websites).

What is 'Your Money Personality'?

Over the past few years, I've been undertaking some fantastic, exciting and groundbreaking research.

It's exciting because it is the key – THE KEY – to successful and straight-forward money management and wealth creation – for every individual.

Exciting because I have developed a unique suite of profiling tools to help people to identify and develop their own personal money management practices – ones that work for and feel right for them.

Exciting because, finally, here is a profiling process which combines mind, head and heart to help and guide people to have, and experience, a rich and abundant life.

We know that identifying our beliefs, attitudes and values is very important to understanding how we make our financial decisions and choices. We know that these beliefs, attitudes and values have been shaped and molded by our external environment; such as our family, our school and friends, our spiritual or religious instruction, our community and culture.

But there is one particular area that I came across that really grabbed me – and still has me by the throat! It's the world of temperament theory or personality type.

It is fascinating because it is comparable to a genetic coding which determines how we take in information and how we make decisions. We have a predisposition to the way we believe things and the way our attitudes work for us in the world. It is at such a deep level. It is comparable to the world of epigenetics. This is where people may have a predisposition to a particular physical disease where if they are exposed to a negative environment for long enough, they may end up getting that disease. The operative word here being 'may'. But where that person experiences a positive environment and keeps healthy and well, they may never experience that particular negative side of their genetic pre-disposition.

Well, temperament is a little bit like that. You might have a pre-disposition to making a lot of money quickly or a lot of money slowly or maybe not being interested in making money at all. You may be interested in understanding how the whole system works and using it to your benefit.

What is wonderful is it confirms that all of us are so different in the way that we approach our financial decision making. How we take in information to do with our finances and money and that whole world is unique to each of us.

The profiling processes we offer can show you what your learned responses, attitudes and beliefs and your financial predisposition are. That is such powerful and empowering knowledge for you to have!

Why is Knowing 'Your Money Personality' Important?

Knowing your predisposition to money is a vital component of your financial life. Please understand, your money predisposition is not something that you can just change by going to a three day workshop, or listening to some talks on your mp3. This is a part of our core makeup. Understanding and learning how to manage it is the key!

Studying the various forms of human temperament has been around for 2,500 years – going back to Hippocrates. Of course, since then, it has been touched upon by numerous different philosophers and psychologists over the years. It was Jung who laid the foundations for bringing it 'main stream' and said that the personality type was the most important discovery of his whole working career.

He was so excited by the possibilities of identifying an individual's personality - which parallels so easily with temperament - which can then be used to achieve personal individuation, or becoming whole.

What are the
'Money Personality' Types?

There are essentially four different money types.

We define them as the Bull, the Bear, the Owl and the Dolphin.

One of the key results to identifying what type we are is that we can get a sense of what is valuable to us, as an individual, and what it is that we need.

As we understand our value, and where we can be of value, and when we can identify the things that are important to us, our self-esteem grows stronger. One of the things we have long observed is that financial success and self-esteem are very closely related.

When you are meeting your needs, you start to feel good about yourself and as you feel good about yourself you feel more prosperous, more confident.

The Bull

There are a lot of very successful Bulls out there that have identified how money works for them. They are the personalities in life who love to find deals to make money.

Often, they also teach others about making money - Robert Kiyosaki and Donald Trump are typical examples of this Bull type.

We admire them for their freewheeling and daring attitude as they invest and leverage as much as they can while taking a lot of commonly perceived risks.

'Commonly' perceived, but the Bull doesn't see much risk at all. They love to start up new businesses and make as much money as they can from selling them off, often at a huge profit.

Get-Rich-Quick scheme promoters often have the Bull temperament too. They are very charismatic and believable and have an exciting bouncy personality while taking advantage of whatever possibilities might come their way.

Share traders and currency and commodity traders fit well in the Bull type also. This is your Gordon Gecko type from the movie 'Wall Street' – showing the freewheeling, daring and charismatic personality.

Bulls enjoy risk, and they are good with taking a lot of risks but sometimes that very fine line between gambling and trading is crossed. This is when losses and bankruptcy take over!

The Bulls have strong material needs. Donald Trump and Robert Kiyosaki are people who are buying and selling businesses, buying and selling properties, wheeling and dealing and having a lot of excitement, a lot of fun. That is what they love to do. Making a lot of money, losing a lot of money and then making it back again; that is the Bull's idea of a rich and rewarding life.

A Bull that is working in their temperament would consider a 'great financial day' to hold the excitement of the big deal - the freedom and the impact that they can make as a result of what they are doing with their money and profits. Bulls love to be in the present moment.

The Bear

The Bear tends to be quite cautious with their money. They also tend to be very good with money. They are the most careful personality with regards to their spending habits but when it comes to investing, they can be a little overcautious particularly around leveraging and borrowing - certainly more than other types.

This is where money management education becomes so important. When a Bear educates themselves about money management and investing, their confidence grows and they become good, steady investors.

It comforts the Bears greatly to understand how asset protection works and how it reduces a lot of investing risk. Once they understand risk and are comfortable around risk (and knowing their money personality type is a big part of that), they are able to make good long term investment strategy decisions that are right for their type. They don't jump onto the next big thing when it comes along.

Bears like to follow the rules. They are happy to follow authority and they like to follow what they know. Your typical Bear would be someone like Warren Buffett, the most successful investor in the world. When everybody was investing in the dotcom sector, Warren Buffett was staying well away.

He was quite clear that this was a bubble and he didn't agree with how the companies and their shares were being valued so highly. By following his gut feeling to stay away and continue to invest safely in what he knew, he didn't get burned like so many others when the dotcom bubble burst and that sector of the market crashed. Buffett was quite happy to allow others to make money or lose money in the dotcom boom and bust. He still made money on the shares and investments that he knew and understood and felt comfortable with.

The Bears have the temperament for doing really well financially and are usually quite good around earning, because they tend to be good business people. They are attracted to business and are quite well regarded as leaders of business. A lot of CEO's are Bears and because of their cautious approach, they are good at making decisions with little or just enough information.

Bears tend to go to the sorts of jobs where they are looking after community and they like to belong to organizations. They tend to stay in careers for long periods of time and Bears tend to be the typical accountant.

A rich lifestyle for a Bear is to be part of a community - where they can belong. Being cautious and being careful, doing what is responsible and stable; in a corporate environment or in another group or community type of environment where they may, or may not, make their way to the top and be a leader.

In that Bear process, they are also buying their own home. They are paying money into their superannuation so that when they retire they have enough money to look after themselves and their family, and do what is important to them; whether that's traveling or just being there for their extended family.

Bears tend to have stronger material needs than Dolphins and Owls, but not quite as much as Bulls. They are attracted to material things and that is part of what makes them feel stable and secure; having material things around them. That is one reason why they do quite well financially.

It is not a bad thing to want to have material things around you. It is more whether you can afford them or not. The Bears would make sure that they could afford them! They would not be investing in something that they couldn't afford. They would most likely have done the numbers or got someone do the numbers for them, and see that they can afford it. This behaviour makes them feel secure. They would buy assets that would 'feed' them with passive income.

The Owl

The Owl tends to make decisions by the numbers. The Owls are just as they are portrayed; intelligent, and wise (although personality is not a measure of intelligence and skill). They like to understand how the system works. They like to use their intellect to understand the numbers and what those numbers mean.

They tend to do well financially and, interestingly, some research shows that Owls (as a group) tend to be some of the youngest retired individuals of all the four temperaments.

Owls are very open to learning and understanding one of the miracles of finance - compounding. One of the most famous Owls, Albert Einstein, once said that "the greatest discovery of his time was compound interest".

They like to use their wisdom of understanding to invest and once they understand the system and they know what they are doing, they usually do quite well financially. They understand that by regularly and consistently investing over a long period of time, they can make an incredible impact on their financial wellbeing.

In terms of earning, they tend to be quite good earners. Some Owls are natural leaders, and can be drawn to the armed forces. They are also good at creating their own companies that are highly technical or theoretical. Other Owls are sometimes so involved in, and focused on, the theories behind making things happen that they lose sight of making money.

They're just more interested in developing their wisdom and their knowledge!

Because they are good at creating plans, they tend to make good savers, good spenders and good investors. They are quite happy taking risks when they have that knowledge on board. Most of them are quite young when they get to that point in their life where they realize that it is important to have money. They are very future focused.

The Owl's 'rich life' is about knowledge and mastery. Perhaps it might be about mastering the knowledge of finance but probably for them it would be mastering the knowledge of any subject that they were really fascinated with. They may go on to be a university lecturer or someone who knows their subject to the highest degree. As a result they usually get paid quite well for that mastery of knowledge.

Because they are future oriented, they want to be independent as that is of a high value to an Owl. They may have their own business.

Typically, it would be one that can run itself, because they understand systems and they can make quite good amounts of money from that process. They enjoy risk so the focus of a 'rich' lifestyle for them may not necessarily be in owning their own home or owning a number of homes. It is more the independence.

Their ideal is a lifestyle where they have cash flow that allows them to do whatever they want, where their investments look after them. They are at the point where they don't need to work, but they can just follow their passion for knowledge and mastery of, and in, a particular area.

Owls are clever and quite complex characters. They have a deep understanding of the need for taking care of the future. Owls can sometimes be quite risky in their investing because they are good with logic and they are good at getting into intricate details of charting, systems, and concepts.

More than any other type, Owls tend to be very future focused. That helps them in their ability to save and invest because they understand that there will be a need for money in the future.

The Dolphin

An interesting perspective about Dolphins and their particular temperament is that they tend to be a little less materialistic in their focus than other types. They are focused on helping others and meaningful causes and, as long as their finances relate to those values, they are good savers.

They can use those causes, and the desire to help others, to make money (and to invest) but sometimes they can get a little off track because they tend to care less about money than their other goals.

When their values don't relate to business per se, money seems to take a back seat. But of course, like all the types, at some point Dolphins realize, usually a bit later in their life, that when it comes to retirement (to be able to follow those pursuits of literature, and art and all that is beautiful and idealistic) they actually need to have some money!

This is when the Dolphins can tend to get a little bit panicky as they realize that they need much more money for their retirement than they thought.

Unfortunately, they are then open to listening to some Bulls who seduce them by saying "Have I got the most exciting opportunity for you".

Dolphins can be so attracted to that excitement the Bulls put out there. And, of course, a Dolphin doesn't have the temperament to follow the investing path of the Bulls. It is easy for a Dolphin, with their idealistic temperament, to believe what they are being told and a lot of Dolphins can be, and are, taken advantage of financially.

So all you Dolphins – beware the get-rich-quick scheme or the "just give me your money and I'll invest it in forex dealing or options trading for you"! Please just walk away and get some good financial education.

Dolphins can be good investors – using their intuition. They just need the grounding of the number crunching skills to round them out.

A 'rich' life for Dolphins is self-realization and integrity. Interestingly enough, Abraham Maslow identified the pyramid of individual's needs – Maslow's Hierarchy of Needs - and he was a Dolphin!

Self-realization is becoming the best that you can be. It is attaining a certain level of self-awareness and deep understanding of yourself, and of others, so that you can make the greatest impact on the planet. For Dolphins, knowing that they are following their purpose and making an impact and that they have got the awareness of themselves and others is so important. So is making that impact in an empathetic and authentic way.

An ideal day for the Dolphins is to feel and experience their quality of life. It is not necessarily lots of riches and expensive things around them. The quality of life they enjoy is deep and meaningful connection and community. They love emotional beauty and having the sense of what is valuable in nature and relationship and meaning.

A message for every Money Personality...

"It is never too late to take control of your money and get it working for you! An abundant, rich life is not only about having millions of dollars in investments – although that's very nice to have - it is as much about the quality of life and having what matters and is valuable – to you.

Prosperity is as much about having a life that makes you feel prosperous as it is about having investments. Some of our clients are multi-millionaires. When they started working with us, they didn't feel prosperous because they were not in touch with their passion. That changed when they identified their Money Personality and connected to what made their heart sing. So you see, a rich and abundant life is not necessarily all about the money!

It is not about how many toys you have, or how many properties you have, or how much you have invested. It is really living a rich life for you, and your own type."

Your Money Personality and Relationships

Money is one of the main causes of relationship breakdown. Whether it's with your spouse, a life partner or business partner.

In 'The Art of War' by Sun Tzu, he explains that by knowing yourself, you will win the war. By knowing your enemy you will win 100 wars.

Now I'm not saying that your partner is the enemy or that you are at war. Though sometimes it may feel or seem that way!

But when you understand your partner's money personality, you will have clarity about the financial issues that are likely to become challenges in your relationship.

When it comes to money and relationships, there is some evidence that Bears and Bulls are attracted to each other. Then it's the Owls and Dolphins who can often be attracted to each other.

The reason? It's mainly because of the way they communicate – in terms of their use of language and the way they take in and process information and ideas.

Bulls and Bears tend to be more focused on tangibles such as the detail of experience and observation. Owls and Dolphins tend to be more focused on intangibles such as concepts, ideas, implications and meaning.

This is where like attracts like.

We also know that opposites attract. Bears and Bulls are opposites, as are Owls and Dolphins.

Bears like the free spirited spontaneity of the Bull and the Bull likes the organized stability and security of the Bear.

Dolphins like the knowledge and wisdom of the Owl and the Owl is captivated by the compassionate sensitivity and integrity of the Dolphin.

While we are attracted to the similarities and differences of our business and marriage or life partners, these attractions can also become the areas of greatest conflict when it comes to money.

By knowing your type, and your partner's type, you can 'walk a mile in the shoes of your partner' without losing your perspective on the situation.

Bears need security and Bulls need freedom. You can see the cause of many a conflict!

While two Bulls may not argue about taking big risks and overspending, issues will arise down the track if these behaviors continue without caution.

Owls and Dolphins will argue over issues of logic versus ideals and personal values. What is right for one partner is not for the other.

Understanding yours and your partner's money personality allows you to accept the different approaches to money matters.

Understanding and acceptance can create harmony which is a great place to discuss common goals and a shared future.

Introducing The Ladder of Abundance™ and How the Money Personality Fits

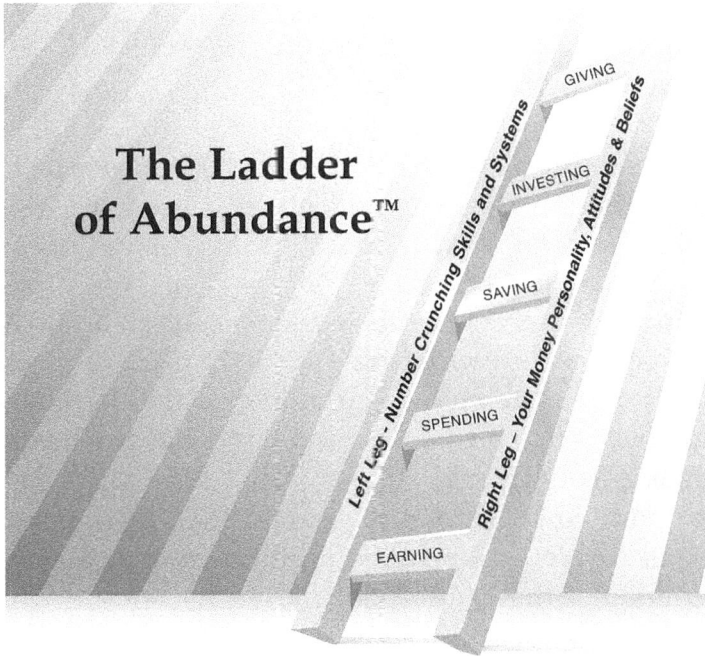

The Ladder
of Abundance™

GIVING

INVESTING

SAVING

SPENDING

EARNING

Left Leg - Number Crunching Skills and Systems

Right Leg - Your Money Personality; Attitudes & Beliefs

The **Ladder of Abundance**™ is our way to show you our processes and components of creating and living an abundant life.

As they say "a picture is worth a thousand words"!

It's like climbing a virtual ladder.

Firstly, there are the two side rails, or legs, of the Ladder. On one side – the left side - we've got the skills, the systems and the financial vehicles, or structures that you are going to use to build your wealth. And on the other side, - the right hand side - are your beliefs, your values and **THE** key; your money personality.

Then, holding those two rails together are the steps. These steps are:

1. **Earning**
2. **Spending**
3. **Saving**
4. **Investing**
5. **Giving**

It's not necessarily that once you have stepped past 'earning' you don't have to think about it anymore. It's more that you have got it in place, and it's the right way of earning for your money personality.

Getting to the top of your ladder means that all these 5 steps/processes are working together, using the correct structures and systems for you, and your ladder is against the right wall – that means you're doing what you love to do; what makes you happy.

The main idea is to put your ladder up against the right wall for you - for your unique personality and your temperament – the key to your individual investment and wealth creation plan.

Now, when I refer to a wall, it's not a negative reference. It's the wall that makes up and is a part of your financial home.

As we discussed before, we have created a tool and processes to identify whether you are a Bull, a Bear, an Owl or a Dolphin. Each one of us will have a preference for one of those four temperaments, with a little bit of the others thrown in just to make it interesting!

When you have identified Your Money Personality, you can be confident that you have put your ladder against the right wall. The wall that is aligned with your personal core needs, values, talents and behaviors, and the wall that is going to be most useful for you to achieve the outcomes of a secure financial future and an abundant, rewarding life.

Your financial money house is a house in which you will

be happy to reside. The house that fulfills all the needs that you have as an individual. This is not somebody else's dream house that you'll be moving into. Sometimes we can get confused. We look around and see somebody else's house that we admire and think, "I'd love to live there". The reality is that if we did live in that house it wouldn't be fulfilling our individual needs.

Over the years; those clients who came to us for help were caught in that trap – wanting someone else's life. They had been spending money on things that didn't give them the real value and fulfillment that they wanted. They were in a never ending cycle of earning and spending, just trying to feel alive and whole. If they hadn't sought our coaching help and they hadn't found out their money personality, they would not have made it to the other rungs of that ladder; the rungs of saving and investing. They would have stayed stuck at the earning and spending steps! This is a cycle that has to be broken, and the only way to break that cycle is having a willingness to change, developing a self-awareness (this is where the money personality comes in), and then – just doing it!

How Knowing 'Your Money Personality' Helps You

You may now be wondering if you are a Bull, a Bear, a Dolphin or an Owl.

When you have your profiling session, you will do the Majors profiling tool which gives you a Myers/Jungian analysis of your personality type. Then, you complete our financial and investing profiling tools. There's every possibility that you may come up as a different financial type to what you thought. This is where financial education comes in!

When a particular money personality type gets a good financial education, their behaviour in the areas of earning, spending, saving, investing and giving can change or can be different and take on the traits of another temperament.

This is true personal growth in the form of a kind of financial individuation.

I think the most obvious one that we have experienced is Dolphins taking on some Bull behaviour when they invest. This is because of the level of education that they have received. This is really exciting! Why? Because the Bulls out there are really making an impact on the financial world in a way I am sure a lot of Dolphins would love to make, solely from a financial perspective.

For example, Louise's (my business partner's) natural personality type is a Dolphin when she does the Jungian/Myers personality profiling. But as far as her investing temperament is concerned, she is a Bull (albeit a more conservative one!). Essentially, a temperament is the indicator of our preferences. We all have different abilities and preferences for using intuitive information, taking in and sensing information. We then process this information (with different personalities processing in different ways) and make decisions from either a thinking and logical perspective or a feeling and values perspective.

Louise is a Dolphin who invests with the free spiritedness and ability to handle risk that the Bull would enjoy. This is because of the many years she spent in the accounting and stock broking industries. Therefore what would seem like risk taking to a Dolphin, is no longer as risky because of her experience and financial education. Such education would include an understanding of the concepts of compounding, leveraging and how markets and economic cycles work.

It is not only education - It's also getting the confidence to start Investing. That's when you really get your lessons. The education is fabulous and gives confidence to start, but there's no substitute for getting out there and actually buying some shares, when appropriate, or buying your first investment property, when it is the right thing for you.

A wonderful way that people to learn about money and investing is to join us and take The Great Cash Flow Challenge. It's a fun day where like-minded people get together and play money games (and no, it's not Monopoly!). It's a great way to fine-tune your financial savvy and you can try being a different Money Personality type and practice those Bull, Bear, Owl or Dolphin behaviour before you actually go out and hit the market. Why not join us? You will meet fabulous people plus learn heaps about money and investing. To find out when and where our next Great Cash Flow Challenge day is, go to our website at www.yourlifeyourmoney.com.au

Once you've got the knowledge and the education, you have the realization that risk isn't what you originally thought it was. You are also aware of what is gambling as opposed to investing. Remember that a full understanding of the difference between gambling and investing is different for each type.

Test your skills. As each of the different types has various skills which they have as a preference, naturally, these are the ones they use most frequently.

However, it's those skills or functions that are referred to as 'inferior', or least preferred, which are the greatest tools to self-development for an individual.

Particularly with Dolphins, when it comes to finance, they can find their greatest level of personal realization and self-realization as a result of mastering their finances or business (if they own one). Getting an understanding of some of the logical planning skills, and being able to see, touch, feel, hear and experience what it is like to invest is activating and developing those 'inferior' functions. This results in them becoming a well-rounded Dolphin!

The key is realizing that there is not a cookie cutter approach to making money. Every personality type does it differently. And the key is that when you know your type, it lets you put your ladder up against the wall that is going to fulfill your needs and the needs that will develop your self-esteem and your self-worth, which will then turn into actual material wealth.

When somebody doesn't manage their own money and investments in accordance with their type, they become exhausted, overwhelmed and stressed. There is also the possibility of self-sabotage – just to stop the pain!

It's worth noting that within the same temperaments – Bears, Bulls, Dolphins and Owls - some are extroverts and some are introverts. And of course, the way an introvert and an extrovert invests can be quite different. Where the extroverts may like to get involved in the particular investment process, an introvert might like to stay well back and not get so involved. Mainly because it might cause them more stress than is necessary, and when under stress they may make decisions that cause them some financial difficulty.

Then within each of the temperaments, they can be broken up into four again - into four types. So there are 4 Bears, 4 Bulls, 4 Owls and 4 Dolphins, and each one of these also has a slightly different way that they 'do' earning, spending, saving, investing and giving!

It is all about understanding your strengths and identifying your challenges so you can manage those challenges in the future around your money management and investing.

The depth of research, and the depth of work we do with clients, is profound. It is not to confuse or overwhelm; it is to enlighten. Clients have said that it was such a relief for them to find out that they could do what they actually loved, rather than feeling they had to do it in some particular way that just didn't fit for them.

Many have also said that they found that when they were true to their to their type with their money management, they discovered they needed a lot less money than they thought they would need, to live that life that was right for them.

That is so freeing and so empowering for all of us as individuals.

Clients have found they experience such lightness when they realized that to have a really fulfilling, wealthy life, they didn't have to live up to the expectations of others.

You've read the eBook, so how about having your profile done? It's one thing to get a feel for what 'Animal archetype' you are, but to really know, and understand, is life changing stuff!

Remember, knowing Your Money Personality will give you great insight into your strengths and how you can use those to experience a rich and abundant life PLUS you will identify the challenges you have around money and earning, spending, saving, investing and giving and you will get help with how to manage those challenges.

Don't worry, we all have the challenges - it's knowing what those challenges are and knowing how to manage them – that's the key!

I look forward to working with you!

Yours Abundantly, JP

Your Gift

'As a special 'Thank you' for purchasing my book and to help you further with your Money Personality education, here's a gift for you – with my compliments!

It's free video training called 'Master Your Money' where you will get further insights into Your Money Personality plus learn how to build your financial foundations – the key to a secure financial future.

It's valued at $97 but it's yours – as my gift.'

You can access it here:

http://yourlifeyourmoney.com.au